ST. PAUL

A GOOD FRIEND OF JESUS

The Life of St. Paul the Apostle

Written and illustrated
by the Daughters of St. Paul

ST. PAUL EDITIONS

ISBN 0-8198-6810-8 paper
ISBN 0-8198-6811-6 plastic

Printed in the U.S.A. by the Daughters of St. Paul
50 St. Paul's Ave., Boston, Ma. 02130

The Daughters of St. Paul are an international congregation of religious women serving
the Church with the communications media.

A long time ago in a faraway land there lived a little boy. The little boy's name was Saul. Saul was a good boy. He loved his mother and father very much.

One day Saul's mother and father sent him to school in the city of Jerusalem. In Jerusalem, there lived a holy man. He told Saul all about God. Saul was very happy. He wanted to love God very much.

Saul was a good boy in school. He studied and he learned to love God very much. He wanted to do everything he could to please God.

But there was one thing Saul did not learn in school. He did not learn about Jesus. When Saul grew up he did not want to hear people talking about Jesus. Because he did not know Jesus, he did not love Jesus. Poor Saul! He soon began to hurt the people who loved Jesus. He put them into jail. Saul thought he was pleasing God by doing this. Saul did not know that Jesus is God.

One day, Saul went to a city called Damascus. He wanted to put into jail the people there who loved Jesus. While he was on his way to Damascus a great light flashed around him. The light was so bright that it blinded Saul. Saul fell down to the ground. He heard a voice, "Saul, Saul, why are you hurting me?" Saul asked: "Who are you, Sir?" The voice answered, "I am Jesus, the one you are hurting." Now Saul understood. When he hurt the friends of Jesus, he was hurting Jesus, because Jesus loves His friends.

Saul got up from the ground. But he could not see. Saul's friends took him by the hand and brought him into the city of Damascus. A holy man named Ananias came to see Saul. He put his hands on Saul's eyes. "Saul," he said, "Jesus, whom you saw on the way to Damascus sent me to help you." He touched Saul's eyes. Saul could see! He got up and was baptized. Now Saul believed in Jesus; now he loved Jesus.

Saul wanted everyone to know about Jesus. So he began to tell the people in Damascus about Jesus. But the people didn't believe Saul. They thought he was just trying to trick them. Some even wanted to hurt Saul. Saul's friends helped him to run away. He went to a desert; there he prayed and studied about Jesus. After a few years he went to the city of Jerusalem. He saw some of Jesus' good friends: Peter, John, and James and the other apostles. After a few weeks Saul went back to his home. There he worked and prayed.

He waited for Jesus to let him know what he could do to help other people love Him.

"Go tell the people about me!" Jesus told Saul, whose name was also Paul. Paul went to many different countries. He told the people all about Jesus. Sometimes he was cold and hungry. Sometimes he had no place to live.

But Paul still went on. He wanted everyone to know about Jesus. Many people listened to Paul.

Often, after Paul left a city, he wrote letters to the people who loved and followed Jesus. He kept telling the people again and again how much Jesus loved them. He told the people how to love Jesus in return, especially by being good to one another. The people kept the letters Paul wrote to them. They read them at their meetings.

One day Nero, who was the Emperor of Rome, heard that Paul was teaching about Jesus. Nero did not like this. So he had Paul killed. Since Paul loved Jesus very much, he was happy to die for Jesus.

Now we call Paul **St. Paul.** The word "saint" means "holy." St. Paul lives with Jesus in heaven, and he is very happy. Let us pray to him. St. Paul will help us to love God. He will help us to be good and to be holy, too.

But there are still people who do not know Jesus, who do not love Him. If we tell our friends about Jesus we will be just like St. Paul. And we also will be good friends of Jesus and of St. Paul.

Daughters of St. Paul

IN MASSACHUSETTS
 50 St. Paul's Ave. Jamaica Plain, Boston, MA 02130;
   617-522-8911; 617-522-0875;
 172 Tremont Street, Boston, MA 02111; 617-426-5464;
   617-426-4230
IN NEW YORK
 78 Fort Place, Staten Island, NY 10301; 212-447-5071
 59 East 43rd Street, New York, NY 10017; 212-986-7580
 7 State Street, New York, NY 10004; 212-447-5071
 625 East 187th Street, Bronx, NY 10458; 212-584-0440
 525 Main Street, Buffalo, NY 14203; 716-847-6044
IN NEW JERSEY
 Hudson Mall — Route 440 and Communipaw Ave.,
   Jersey City, NJ 07304; 201-433-7740
IN CONNECTICUT
 202 Fairfield Ave., Bridgeport, CT 06604; 203-335-9913
IN OHIO
 2105 Ontario St. (at Prospect Ave.), Cleveland, OH 44115; 216-621-9427
 25 E. Eighth Street, Cincinnati, OH 45202; 513-721-4838
IN PENNSYLVANIA
 1719 Chestnut Street, Philadelphia, PA 19103; 215-568-2638
IN FLORIDA
 2700 Biscayne Blvd., Miami, FL 33137; 305-573-1618
IN LOUISIANA
 4403 Veterans Memorial Blvd., Metairie, LA 70002; 504-887-7631;
   504-887-0113
 1800 South Acadian Thruway, P.O. Box 2028, Baton Rouge, LA 70821
   504-343-4057; 504-343-3814
IN MISSOURI
 1001 Pine Street (at North 10th), St. Louis, MO 63101; 314-621-0346;
   314-231-5522
IN ILLINOIS
 172 North Michigan Ave., Chicago, IL 60601; 312-346-4228
IN TEXAS
 114 Main Plaza, San Antonio, TX 78205; 512-224-8101
IN CALIFORNIA
 1570 Fifth Avenue, San Diego, CA 92101; 714-232-1442
 46 Geary Street, San Francisco, CA 94108; 415-781-5180
IN HAWAII
 1143 Bishop Street, Honolulu, HI 96813; 808-521-2731
IN ALASKA
 750 West 5th Avenue, Anchorage AK 99501; 907-272-8183
IN CANADA
 3022 Dufferin Street, Toronto 395, Ontario, Canada
IN ENGLAND
 57, Kensington Church Street, London W. 8, England
IN AUSTRALIA
 58 Abbotsford Rd., Homebush, N.S.W., Sydney 2140, Australia